REFLECTIONS

REFLECTIONS

Poems from a regular dude!

Ju-San

Library of Congress Control Number:		2018906654
ISBN:	Hardcover	978-1-9845-2971-8
	Softcover	978-1-9845-2970-1
	eBook	978-1-9845-2969-5

Print information available on the last page.

Rev. date: 06/21/2018

To order additional copies of this book, contact:
Xlibris
1-888-795-4274
www.Xlibris.com
Orders@Xlibris.com
779944

Contents

INTRODUCTION

Some would say its a little dark, some would say it is sad. A tapestry of both sewn together to express ones thoughts that he has had. The split in personality from melancholy to some stories of inspiration to even a little humor. Like art some will make sense and others wont. But that is the point is to leave it open for the readers mind to decide how it relates to them personally. Will they understand the gesture the words translate and convey into? An open ending for a story of ones life told in a somber sentences. Follow with an open mind.

This book can be used as a read or journal. Blank lines have been added for the convenience of the reader to add notes or thoughts related to the poem or their personal life.

DEDICATION

This book is dedicated to my children Vanessa, Raven, Lyana, Trinity and Tristan (my twins).

These words inside this book are my feelings of what I've felt in my existence.

My own struggle, my own pain, the good and the bad things that I have seen and witnessed.

In my life time I have:

Been hurt by those that I've trusted (so called friends) but I have also hurt people.

I've been belittled and put down.

I've experienced things that a young kid should have never experienced.

I've begged, borrowed and stolen from people.

I've lied and cheated.

I've ruined two marriages.

I am a lot of things but the devil I am not.

I live with a grave and sincere regret and darkness that I battle and try to balance in my days.

My childhood is a glimpse of internal thought. Can't tell if my dreams were dreams or faded memories.

I have been through abuse (not from my mother), foster homes, a runaway counseling, jail several times as a kid, the streets, bounced from school to school due to my unwelcomed and unacceptable behavior. The list goes on.

This book does not explain my life as a child but my thoughts and feelings as a man.

Walk with me into my pain and mind.

It started from someplace...

September 29,2014

A placid man once asked a fellow passerby while he walked on a long road venturing through time,"what do you want in life"? Confused by his question he responded with, "i'm not sure, its never crossed my mind". Not surprised by the latters response, he replies, "we walk this road not knowing whats before the next step but we take a chance on our journey". The young man awakens in a slight panic. He looks around only to notice no ones there. "It must have been a dream", he gently whispers! He picks up his affects by the tree and proceeded to his unknowing destination. Bothered by this dream he begins to consider what was said. He thinks to himself, "You never know when you will be faced with yourself". How do you address each other? He begins to question "What have i done in my life to know what i want"? Still on his journey he finds a comfortable spot by a wired fence and a hay stack to rest for a while. Still bothered by his own question he looks around and notices some farm animals and realized how they serve only one purpose. Still looking he sees some other animals and some birds and an owl. His journey has clearly made him fatigued. He falls asleep only after a short while, a voice begins to echo "Who are you, are you free from burdens"? Again he is awaken by a voice. He looks around again, still notices the animals, birds and that owl. The owl turns a blind eye. He studies his surrounding for a moment. Realization kicks in! "Unlike the animals behind the fence we all have a choice to go somewhere and do something" he says to himself! Amazed on his enlightment that has been bestowed upon him he decides to turn back around and go back to the beginning...Ju-San SO TELL ME PEOPLE, WHAT DOES THIS MEAN TO YOU?

September 21,2015

Lets navigate together through the ocean sky while stars drip below us for a smooth tide.

I see before me a destiny that's filled with things only I see.

So lets get together for a rendezvous and have some fun with friends, family, me and you.

Tickets are being sold quick for this ride in my paradise so you better hurry if you want to take this flight.

Fasten your seat belt, the conductor has arrived. Time to punch your ticket and sail through my eyes.

WAIT! This would only be true if I had someone to call ME and YOU.

Well, I guess I'm riding solo, so if anyone tries to take this extra seat that would be a NO NO.

A stranger perhaps would be good to converse with in syllables and vocabulary coming from swift lips.

Ahhh, how sweet and fluid do those verbs explode with compound expression as you breath out your nose. Energized as lighting soring in the tapestry of clouds. Radiant and vibrant!

Time to accelerate and move forward with my journey. No brakes for me for I will not stop. Run away horse with high speed torque.

I'll see you when I see you, Its time to go!

I hope you grasp my meaning, if not, well then, SO!

HAHAHA...Ju-San

June 30, 2015

Times of sorrow, hate, racism, and lost of faith.

Gather together as the sun in morning holding forever in the rivers dawn.

Where is the love for my fellow man that we've all lost in confusion?!? When do we set aside the bad energy and rid of this anarchy that we yearn for taste!? Behold as the hate is slowly creeping to our hearts just waiting for the trigger to start firing. Time will slow down for us all! Descending to the ground when it all falls into crumbles. Tears, mourns and whispers of mumbles. When do we STOP just for a moment to understand ourselves and further educate from books on the shelves? Draw your own opinion! LETS CREATE A BETTER HISTORY TO REDEFINE HIS-STORY!

Let's show that we can change together and write a our own definition of life. For words have no meaning if you so choose to not define who we are.

I will give you a place to contemplate your thoughts and feeling without mistake.

Where you stand now is your home. Decide to deviate you will forever roam into space.

Can we do this? YES, of course! So as long as we set aside opinions and what we think we know. Take the time and go learn for yourself and not follow social media that we've bestowed upon ourselves. The sun doesn't judge the water. The water doesn't judge the sun. But every day from dusk till dawn they touch each other's face with good reason...Ju-San

P.S. We all need to believe in ourselves and in each other. Be caring and be kind! Mentor and educate our children. We pass the torch and die so they can continue our journey and legacy and so forth. BE WELL AND LIVE!...Ju-San

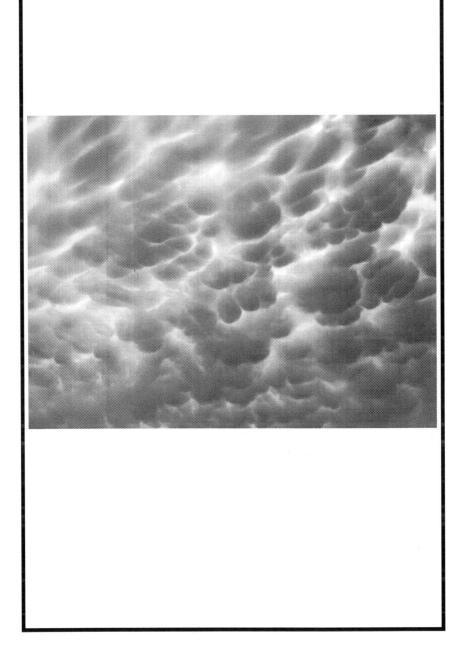

September 18, 2014

A silent cry that can't be heard. This lesson is warranted but I wasn't served. It's dangerous to leave me hear alone in my room to roam dazed and confused, I'm gone!

Going down upwards in a stage of flight, the mirror is backwards, I've left this sight. I can't right this wrong when knowing all along that I've become sensitive to this poem.

I steered away from the path of enlightenment, I've lost my way. It's time to go back to the beginning where and when I was left astray. The light dimmed in the silhouette of time, I must return. To my lessons of life when it was yearned. I think I will go back to a little of who I was, when the path was straighter and as clear as the sky above...Ju-San

September 18,2014(4)

What is wrong? Why do your eyes comply as the sky falls in wet solitude? Latter feels this hurt of depression and loneliness. Tired of equated as a libertine and left with brokenness. But thee is who enjoys the small pleasures of acting without moral restraint. Astounded by his own response, he is with no complaint.

I feel as though my purpose is incomplete and has not yet begun. The mirage blinds my decisions from what's real, this is no fun!

A flower with no water can not grow and blossom to show it's true colors. Without thought it just IS. It is what it was meant to BE. BEautiful! Go seek out what is meant to be for who you are is? A vague question with an answer lost in the abyss...Ju-San

_____

_____

_____

_____

_____

_____

_____

_____

_____

_____

_____

_____

_____

September 18,2014(2)

The reflections in the mirror, the sight that stares. The silent sighs, no one hears. Numbness through my body my hands can't grasp. Weakness in my knees my body can't stand. The scarlet runs, it flows through my veins, as the tears fall again and again. No feeling of what once was. The eyes are in full moon, as the words are hush. Its all too soon. The body fades rapidly through the wine river, the warmth is getting cold, the body is in shivers. My apology to you, the one I don't see. My strength was taken, in ways it can't be...Ju-San

September 18,2014(3)

THE UNTITLED WORDS.

Who is in this room with me? I only ask because I can not see you. As this room is filled with darkness it has left my mind filled with the welcoming of death. I am only left with a small lit candle and a box of matches. In a glance I notice a rope by a door. I scream and yell "NO MORE"! Only the door has no handles or hinges or window. No one to acknowledge my screams. How did I get in here? Is suicide my freedom, my way out? But why the rope? No place to hang it. The thought of this rope is torturing me. But in a twisted nurturing way its my companion. What should I call it? Maybe I'll call it CHOKE or maybe HOPE! Yeah, that's what I'll call it. HOPE! Ironically it briefly made me forget about where I was at. Reality is back in the presence of time. Time and Space. Time and Space. My time in this space. This empty void of endless walls. That door, this rope. I wish it all would go away. What is on the other side? This door that exist before me is a lie. Maybe nothing on the other side. This door separates what could be REAL. The world of the known and unknown. But to which do I exist in? This damn rope. TELL ME WHAT DO YOU WANT FROM ME?!?!?! Sighs, whimpers, slow heavy breaths. I'm sure you know the rest...Ju-San

_____

_____

_____

_____

_____

_____

_____

May 2018

Pen,
why do you dislike me?
Why do you write in transparency?
Do I transcend above your literary?
I've only tried to become what's fair to see.
In time you will realize that we have much in common.
We both think alike.
We both feel what's inside.
We both know each other's eyes.
The bleeding of the soul that's told us so, In our face with shame
and disgrace.
I'm rambling through with no sense or understanding, no clue.
I've falling from where I was standing just to plead your beg.
You've tried to please our mind without any legs.
On knees I'm bare with words not yet written there.
What's more to say?
I'm running out of letters to put together.
This verbal tapestry has unstitched
from its unwritten header.
Where do I begin the title from above?
This ending had exhausted the ink in vein.
Sinful words with spaces of plain text.
Who knows what's next!?
Do I continue to solder time with paper in mime?
The third has battled the latter with the mad hatter.
Now we have taken a twist in spoken lisp in ties of tongue.
The unpronounced is foreign to my grammar in vocabulary
riddle with no glamour, yet to be hung.
This sentence is killing me in sane mind at the same time insane
in rhyme that has me drinking wine to numb my mind as I whine.
Rambling again…Ju-San

October 27, 2014

Good morning to all in the world of FB. Have a very positive and productive day. Don't let anyone or anything stand in your way of your daily accomplishments. Surround yourselves with positive energy and push away the negative. BE MAGNETIC! You rise and shine and blossom in your mind. Love all and believe in yourself. YOU ARE ALL BEAUTIFUL! Your destiny starts where you make that first step. BE HUMBLE and MOVE FORWARD!...Ju-San ♥

October 7, 2014

A place beyond the pines is where the feeble man stands on this land to find that nothingness exist in the minds of the empty minded.

But the mind is never empty! What is empty is the thought of emptiness.

Some how this makes no sense at making sense at all.

Does my existence remain with cause? The quarry has been inquired by the inquiries of this man in pause.

I speak in riddles as my voice is my instrument although at times i try to instruct and rid of this lament. Unsuccessful, he was fluent in his influence as the desire died with my foment. Influenced by the influence of others!

In a sense, i was innocent while some people are blinded by their own ignorance.

I transition these words of tapestry and emotion. I dialect my notion in a verse of a conceptual hearse. i curse the day of my death. My words are not loud enough as i remain wordless.

What is the message being conveyed, the nights are lonely dark and gray?!?

Drop to his knees as he begs for his plea. A feeling of guilt as he's not yet pleased. Pleasant may be this feeble man as he continues to question whats at hand. A question unasked is a question unanswered by the person who already knows.

Where do i go from here?

Well, not so much of where i'm going but whats coming to me without knowing?!?...Ju-San

August 31, 2017

Words are puzzled together to create musical collision as it collides through the strings and notes for the sound of beauty...Ju-San

_____

_____

_____

_____

_____

_____

_____

November 19, 2015

I'm here, you're there. The universe is everywhere. I'm ok, youre great. Time is in this space. Your pleasant smile, my goofy charm. Indeed, in your arms.

Psst, shall we go? I don't know! Let's take a chance. This is not a novelty or romance but merely a sight to see for a simple dance. Yes, maybe a rockabilly of swinging gesture or a simple touch of slow tunes to impress her. Sweat down the brows of either or! Let's make the earth shake as we tremble the floor.

WAIT! Who am I kidding, who do I speak of? Wouldn't you like to know?

Well, duuh, yeah!...until the next words are spoken, Farewell and goodnight, the eyes are shut in the sky with hoping...Ju-San

November 4, 2014

What is it that you want?
When and where do I start?
Why does this exist
Who are you now?
How does it end???
The answers are in the questions... Belonging to something in life, Being who you are, Becoming one with your inner self, key word...BE!...Ju-San

_____

_____

_____

_____

_____

_____

_____

_____

_____

_____

_____

_____

_____

_____

_____

_____

November 17,2014

To accept imperfection in a person is to accept for what we are,
Our nature is not contemporary for it is by far.
The mirror reflects an image manifested in our own minds,
Our eye sees the truth in all due time.
The meaning of your existence is a subtext put in words,
Im back in the beginning never to be heard.
My words crash like waves speaking uncertain sounds,
If you dont know what im saying, dont leave, stick around.
I follow the steps before me unaware of whats left behind,
The door opens slowly, the gesture is just to kind.
Im awake as my eyes are open,
But my mind is still asleep,
My mouth opens in elegy, the words i cant repeat.
Hidden in the depths of a blackened void,
This challenge i cant deny,
Attempting to recreate myself the image is so fine.
I thank you now for taking the time to read from my hand,
I know if you dont get what is simply said, this i understand. Ju-San

_____

_____

_____

_____

_____

_____

_____

_____

_____

_____

_____

November 17,2014

Theses words are illusions coming out my pen-spilling from the universe i feel cursed again.
Time waits for no one when comes the end-if i continue to write when will i begin?
A friend told me once that life is laughter-here is what i said a few minutes after.
Here is what i say to you in a soliloquy of words-if i continue to write when will my letters be heard?
Dark does not write the words on this page-moments of silence is what i feel some days.
The scarlet fades in the inner hourglass-must keep on writing or the time will pass.
Is my head filled with this magnitude of lies?-or am i just a soul waiting to pass by?
The lines of this elegy gets smaller by day-must continue to write what i feel he says.
Im not trying to mock my own thoughts-im just running out of time by the hands of the clock.
So forgive me now if i dont share the same humor-cant wait till my end, wish it would come sooner.
You might think that this poem is on death-but i assure you that this is not at my best.
If i wrote the words that the others breath-there would be plenty of me to be seen.
Because my dirge is a song of mournful play-i dont expect for you to understand some things that i say.
So back to the beginning is where i will end-these words are illusions coming out my pen...
Ju-San

October 5,2017

Oh how thee sways forth and back in search of the truth. The words lack with definition specified in how I choose.
I see thou face is lathered in tears that ink in this tapestry of letters.
More and more he continues to get better in his own meaning of whats wailed. The moon is pail as it hangs alone in this nakedness of my eye.
Do I forget the advise given to the latter when he is in such emotion?
My imperfections has lashed for my sins. Chastised for it again and again. I have punished thee since the end as it begins by the hands of my own award.
I have given a glance of my own time that perchance it will inevitably make its way back to its place. I am in stasis, unable to move. Surrounded by guilt with much to prove. It's dangerous to be left alone when the crown is gone from the throne.
I don't feel remembered, where has my existence been? Was I that transparent that no one saw me? Apparently!
Where does this end and from what dimensional time, when?
In this court in my own defense as I'm judged in the right hands of what I did wrong...Ju-San

_____

_____

_____

_____

_____

_____

_____

_____

_____

_____

2001

A feeble man walks this land, he is in shame.
A feeble man walks this land, he has no name.
A feeble man walks this land, with no vanity.
A feeble man walks this land, with no life to be…Ju-San

2001(10:45am)

Sleep now for your apathy will let you rest,
You have mustered your last breath,
eyes closed, and body lays erect.
Quantum leap through time,
your body is in mime.
Let yourself be free and return to what you think is serenity.
Its 10:45,
take a breath,
you have just awakened from death...Ju-San

2001

Have you really looked into a person's eye's?
They don't lie of true feeling's.
Look deep into his being,
And see his true meaning.
His hands tremble,
And his skin is cold.
Body is weak,
As it gets old.
Scorned from passerby's,
Eyes wet from a far cry.
A sound of hunger has set in,
What's on today's daily menu special?
While he searches the dumpster from within.
Looks for a dry spot to sit.
Finds a tree,
offers comfort I shall admit.
Blankets himself with grass and leaves.
No one cares to help,
This is what he sees.
Tomorrow will offer something better,
As he sleeps in yelp.

2001(On the corner)

Day 3 of the week,
A man plays his trombone.
Across the street a poor woman dances to his music with joy and
alone.
Day 4, a black woman and a white man going opposite ways,
Stops for a quick kind gestures of hands,
On this sunny day,
Seconds of joyful words exchanged with a smile as they meet.
Going and leaving work,
As they stop for a quick greet.
The time has come for that moment has gone by,
They hug with a simple kiss,
As they smile in bliss,
And wave goodbye...Ju-San

_____

_____

_____

_____

_____

_____

_____

_____

_____

_____

_____

_____

_____

_____

2010(1)

THIS PAIN THAT YOU HAVE CAUSED WILL BE A PART OF YOU FOR YEARS TO COME. ACCEPT IT, EMBRACE IT. FEEL WHAT IT'S LIKE TO BE EMBARASSED AND HUMILIATED. YOU CHOSE THIS WALK OF PATH, THIS IS YOUR WAY TO YOUR FINDING. YOU DO NOT DESERVE THEM NOR DO THEY DESERVE THIS TORMENT YOU HAVE BESTOWED UPON THEM. THE ANGELS EYE'S ARE CRYING INSIDE, SHE WONDERS," WHY HAVE YOU DONE THIS TO US"? WE'RE WE NOT GOOD ENOUGH FOR YOU? UNANSWERED QUESTIONS. YOU WILL SUFFER AS THEY HAVE SUFFERED. DROWN IN THERE TEARS, OPEN YOUR EYES TO THERE FEARS, WITH OPEN HANDS. DO NOT PUSH IT AWAY, CONSUME IT! ACCEPT IT AS A HOMELESS MAN ACCEPTS MONEY FROM A STRANGER, FOR THAT IS YOUR FATE IF YOU CHOOSE TO CONTINUE THIS MENDACIOUS LIFE-STYLE. YOU WILL BE ALONE IN THE END AND YOUR ONLY COMPANION ARE YOUR MEMORIES OF LIES AND DECIET. THAT WILL BE YOUR ONLY FRIEND, THE ONE WHO WILL ALWAYS BE THERE UNTIL DEATH HAS COMFORT YOU WITH OPEN ARMS. COLD AND DARK! I'VE DEVOURED MYSELF TO THE END OF NOTHINGNESS! THIS QUICKSAND WILL NOW BE YOUR HOME! NO ONE TO HELP, YOUR ALL ALONE. NO FORGIVENESS IS TO BE BEGGED FOR, UNTAMED LIES AS ALWAYS, TORN. NO SHEEP IS TO BE HARMED AGAIN...NEVER...NO MORE! YOUR SERENITY HAS MISTED AWAY IN HEAVY WIND AND RAIN. THERE TEARS OF SWEET INNOSCENCE HAS FALLEN ONLY TO DROWN YOU IN THERE IGNORANCE, IF THEY ONLY KNEW THE TRUE YOU! LEFT IN SILENCE, FOR THAT WILL BE YOUR TRUE COMPANY, YOUR PRIVATE BUSINESS. NO BREATH OF HOPE, FOR YOU HAVE WASTED IT ALL.. SHE GAVE YOU ALL HER TRUST AND YOU TURNED HER BACK ON YOU SO SHE COULDN'T SEE YOUR VICE. SO IS IT NOW GOOD BYE OR JUST QUESTIONS WHY? YOUR SELFISHNESS HAS CAUSED UNCONDITIONAL PAIN IN THE HEART!

WHAT IS THE REASON FOR THIS LUST OF WOMEN THAT YOU SO DESPERATELY NEED THERE COMPANY? MISERY WILL GREET YOU ONE DAY AND NO WOMEN WILL FEEL ANYTHING, FOR IT WAS ALL FUN AND GAMES FOR THEM ALSO. THOUGHTS, MEMORIES, CONSTANT REGRETS, WILL HAUNT YOU AS THE DEAD TO A GRAVE. WHEN IS IT ENOUGH? WHEN WILL THIS HUNGER BE FULLY SATSFIED? JUST FUCKING GO AWAY ALREADY, CAN'T YOU SEE THE PAIN SHE IS GOING THROUGH? SHE NEEDS A MAN THAT'S GOING TO BE THERE FOR HER AT ALL TIMES AND COMFORT HER WHEN IN DIRE NEED OF A FRIEND. LETS NOT GO THERE WITH YOU. YOU REALLY FUCKED UP THIS TIME YOU DUMB ASS PIECE OF SHIT! AM I WORTH SAVING? PROBABLY NOT! DROWN IN MISERY! BURN IN HELL! IT AWAITS YOU. AM I THAT BAD OF A PERSON TO DESERVE SUCH TREATMENT? DO I DARE ASK SUCH A QUESTION OR DID SHE EVER SO PASSIONATELY FEEL NOTHING BUT LOVE THAT YOU TOOK FOR GRANTED FOR ME? WHO WILL BE THERE FOR ME? ALL ALONE NOW, LEFT IN MISERY. THE MAN WHO WALKS ALONE! TIME TO FIND YOUR TRUTH! FIND WHERE YOU ARE, FOR YOU ARE LOST. SALVATION? NOT HERE!...JU-SAN

Today 9:37 PM

Babies ok ?

Helllooooo

Delivered

Don't text me. Run to the bottle like always. I need you out of my house. You're 40 trying to act like a kid. Everything about you disgust me. I can't be in the same house as you. You fail in life because of the stupid choices you make. I can't deal with you. You're surrounded by demons. You live for sin & I can't have you around me or my kids!! I refuse to be embarrassed or humiliated by you.

2010(2)

EVERY TIME I LIE, I FEEL THE BLACK LEATHER WHIPPING ME WITH DISGRACE AS THE BLOOD SIGNS THE PAVEMENTS FACE. WITH HASTE I FALL TO MY KNEES AND PLEAD FOR FORGIVENESS, IT ALL STARES BACK AT ME. THE FALL ALONE DOES NOT HURT AS MUCH AS THE HEARTBREAK, FALLEN 2 STORIES TO TELL MY SIDE. I'VE LOST MYSELF A LONG TIME AGO. I DON'T BELIEVE MYSELF WAS A PART OF ME. SINCE INFANCY THERE HAS BEEN ONLY IMAGES OF NOTHINGNESS! DO I REFLECT WHAT I'VE SEEN? AM I THE FALLEN ANGEL LOST BY FAITH? BLEEDING RED RUM! RAIN YOUR BLOOD TO LATHER MY BODY, TOMORROW MY DEATH WILL BE A SONG OF SORROW. THOSE IN MY LOVE WILL YEARN FOR THE GRAVE OF TOMORROWS DAY. AS I FLY TO THE MOUNTAIN SKY, I AM PUSHED AWAY ONLY TO BE DENIED. I HAVE BEEN DESSERTED ON THIS EARTH WITH NOTHING BUT TIME. WHAT IS MY PURPOSE? WHAT IS MY REASON? WAIT A MINUTE, MAYBE ALL THIS THAT I'M GOING THROUGH IS MY UNPAID DEED. UN-REALISTIC!!! OR MAYBE AS I LISTEN AND WATCH THE CROWS SING TO FLOWERS IS A SIGN OF...HOPE!!! SIGNS, THEY CAN GUIDE AND MISGUIDE YOU IN THE WRONG DIRECTION. MY IMAGES AND THOUGHTS ARE MY OWN REALITY. THEY HAVE COME TO LIFE ONLY TO HAUNT ME. WHO IS ACTUALLY IN CONTROL? I ASK! I'VE LOST MY WAY, MUST FIND THE DOOR TO THE OTHER SIDE. OTHER SIDE OF WHAT? THE TRUTH! WHO'S GOING TO HEAR MY CRIES!? WHEN I TELL IT ALL GOODBYE, THE BLACKENED EYES CAN'T SEE FORTH NO MORE, ONLY WHAT IS NOW. HOW DOES ONE TELL IT ALL BEFORE HE FALLS? THE STITCHES INSIDE ARE TEARING APART, TRYING TO HOLD IT TOGETHER, BUT THE HEART IS TOO WEAK TO DEFEAT THIS BATTLE. WITHOUT EYES THERE IS NO TRUTH, NO ENTRY TO THE SOUL, MY EYES ARE NOT WINDOWS TO HEAVEN, SO WHO KNOWS MY REALITY? MY THOUGHTS BLEED SHALLOW WORDS. HOW

CAN I MESSAGE THE PAIN? THESE MINDLESS THOUGTS, THAT I HAVE FOUGHT AND GAINED FOR YEARS, ONLY TO CONVINCE AND SAY WHAT THE HELL AND DO IT. DO WHAT? THESE MENDACIOUS THOUGHTS! WHICH WAY CAN I SWAY? NO TIME TO SPARE FOR THIS DESPAIR THAT I FEEL. UNABLE TO HEAL! HOW LONG MUST I DEAL WITH THESE FEELINGS THAT ARE IN MY HEAD? THE IMAGES OF THIS DISTURBED SOUL WHILE HE RUNS WITH NO PLACE TO GO. IT'S THE BLOODSHED OF HIS PEACE. I'M STUCK IN MY OWN PRISON, UNABLE TO GET OUT AND BE SET FREE. THE HANDS ON MY HEAD TRYING TO HOLD MY THOUGHTS TOGETHER. THE TRUTH IN MY EYES ARE DEFINED. I'VE MADE MY OWN HISTORY, A HISTORY OF PAST FAILURES. LYING IN SILENCE…Ju-San

2012

I'd like to know what I was going through when I wrote this his in 2012

This came up on my "My memories on FB"...

We all know that every once in a while i will post some type of prose writing/poetry so to speak...well this time it will be a little different. here it is; i have just recently experienced something and things that has opened my eyes to some truth about life, relationships, friendship and TRUST etc. well i have decided that due to these recent unexpected and unfortunate events that i will to seek salvation on a higher pillar of my OWN faith in my OWN way. ive been under a lot of false hopes and mis-lead. their has been certain some bodies that i have felt something for at different time periods of my life only to get hurt. truth is, the SHIT SUCKS! we all can relate! so i have decided that i will stay away for awhile from certain things. in this time of my life who will heal the wounded WHO IS ON HIS KNEES BEGGING FOR A PLEAD. the young libertines who only seek for things that is left for the imagining. metaphorically you shall try to understand what words this pen writes from the hand. DOES IT MAKE ANY SENSE? thats the point! LIFE DOES NOT AT TIMES. some of you personnaly know what im talking about and some of you dont. CURIOSITY! such a mind boggle. let rest at peace the the negative in our lives. burry it in the depths of leviathan! LIFE'S ENTRUSTING BEHAVIOR IS DWELLED ON THE SOCIAL ADDICTS OF NOTHINGNESS. just for kicks and giggles, i have no idea what that means. i just made it up and it sounded good... LMAO...but maybe that is the point as well is to CREATE YOUR OWN SOCIAL DEVELOPEMENT. i have allowed myself to put up a brickwall around the heart and to remove one at a time when i thought it was safe. well guess what happened? NOT! the same bricks that i removed were thrown at me. ITS ALL ABOUT THE HIDDEN MESSAGE MY DEAR FB FRIENDS. i can go on and on with this creative mind who thinks of values and morals all the time. but my watch is broken so therefore only unsung words are spoken. i am saying goodbye to FB for awhile. this is my new challenge to myself. i will only use it to keep up with all of you. so in the meantime, LOVE, APPRECIATE and BE GRATEFUL with what you do have especially that speacial someone that you go home to. COMPLIMENT and PRAISE each other. here is my last TAOIST story to you: a man was seeking for poetry in the world so he decided to buy a book that would contain such information. when time went by he realized that LIFE itself was all the poetry he needed. (thats the short version). so until we meet again, THE MAN of the hour has taken his final bow, The curtains come down, i feel that this is JUST GOODBYE for now...

P.S. I will be able to be reached on my FB INBOX if you dont have my phone number to text me. if any of you respond to this post i will respond back as to not to leave you hanging. TAKE CARE MY FRIENDS!...Ju-San

2013

2013 in Lafayette when I wrote this.

I just felt like writing so I decided to write here, figured this is where we all share all our thoughts, feelings and fear. so I will begin to write a short story about IDK, just know that idk which way this will go take a moment and listen(or in this case, read) to my words, because again there is a message that needs to be heard the message so far is what you make of it, its like art in a gallery, expression less you must understand my way of thinking and my sound, before you make judgment of what im texting down so to flip to the other side of what you usually ignore, is that im not making any sense but these words are sojourn if you think you have an idea of what this means, then respond to this of what you think it may seem it may seem that im not sure, but I am sure that this is MY PANACEA(my cure) don't try and ask WEBSTER what these words mean, because my life is like my own dictionary I give it my own meaning from a-z, the rest is in between, YOU CAN NOT SEE your eyes are blinded as a mouse to a trap, victims we are, at night with a bat my time has come to let free this mind, I shall sleep until my alarm unwinds. I will awaken when the time has come for me, to be a part of you again when necessary... Ju-San

_____

_____

_____

_____

_____

_____

_____

2013(2)

Have you ever noticed how calm the night air can be!? Just take that moment and look at what's to be seen. What's to be seen is what we are missing. The grass is wet but yet full. The pavement echoes in silence! The shadow is my only companion, it walks with thought and madness. Watch the cars drive by towards their destination with one thing on their mind no hesitation. This evening is as beautiful as birth for I am feeling alive as I smirk. These city blocks seems as endless as the sky leaving what's behind and waiting to see before. I shall walk some more! I am telling you a story not a folklore. Words are puzzled together! Give it time, and close your mind, the picture will last forever. One day it will be time For me to go home, until then i shall remain and roam. GODSPEED to all! For your journey has only just begun!...Ju-San

2018

Do explain that I do not intrigue you into a mutual conversation?
You sneak a peek at words I do not speak but text on font for a humiliation.
Does she grasp my meaning, or does she choose to ignore feelings of being denied?
I cannot lie, I wish upon you to converse in a conversation that I will commence first.
But wait, what is commenced may not make any sense.
Will she be Au fait with my lingo I express in face?
Ooooh, how sweet you smell with flowers in your hair. As radiant as the sun that rains its shine with all fair.
Me lady, I speak with eloquent and simple understanding.
I shalt not walk away without you demanding.
Your stature is within grasp not to unfold.
You free me as loose leaf drained without words untold.
If you shall disclose correctly a moment of time is what I ask.
Never will you wonder and question what is masked.
Aware that you will pardon me the gratitude and indulge me in your humor.
Profound are your eyes as the oceans tides in depth.
Piercing my lungs as you suffocate me with your given death.
Breathless, as I drown, you push me further down.
All I see is your sweetness within thee.
I am not in fear of what's near to come. It is only time now.
Your scent is all I acquire as I commence to bellow like a choir.
For now, I am breathless!
I suffocate in words to express this emotion I feel in her.
Express lee!...Ju-San

April 23, 2015

Here are some quotes of mine for your daily value:

- To live life in truth and harmony one must deny and rid of all negativity.
- Accept things for what they truly are but don't accept it for what it is. For in life things CAN change.
- Be in the present but present who you are.
- Knowledge is great but when do you apply its value? DO NOT WASTE IT!
- Live a fruitful life! If not the fruit will rot.
- Walk with pride but don't be cocky. Arrogance is unattractive.
- Be bold in your word when speaking your mind but know when to listen. One good ear is worth more than a thousand words.
- Take the time to enjoy the Zephyr wind, it'll clear your mind.
- Limitation vs Capability! Good to know them.
- If you believe you can achieve, you are successful. With success, you are victorious!

Appreciate who you are for there is only one of you. You are special in ways others can not conceive. You are beautiful to those that matters. The latters don't. Perceive who you want to be and BE just that...Ju-San
Live on and live well!

_____

_____

_____

_____

_____

_____

April 5, 2018

Through its time in the ground, it echoes without sound. The rock sits silently. Moved here, moved there, it is camouflaged with its surrounding.

No infliction to itself, pain does not exist.

It can hold weight in its patient place. It is one in the mist.

It time it will diminish and shed its dust. For this is nature and a must.

You cannot throw yourself without aid. Tossed and turned it has returned, again it lays.

Everything has its place.

Its smooth and sharp tone, rhythm when in roam.

It notes its musical play.

Do you pose in solidarity amongst the union?

Those that walk near clap in foot without conclusion.

Offered by its stability and tapestry in collection.

Are you the strength that keeps us whole in our reflection?

Chiseled in stature you etch the ground in artistic pros.

The invisible sun does not shade to you.

Hard rock in a hard place sizzled in stew.

Blinded by rays its kisses and lays in time overdue.

You are of age in time of wisdom, you are one in a few...Ju-San

---

August 12, 2014

This one was dated 8-12-2014 for <u>Craig Wilson</u>. I remember he was going through something personal at the time so I wrote this for him.

    This is for my friend/co-worker Craig Wilson. Hope it all works out for you bro. The river runs through with out judgement or concern of what exist in the now. It spares no thought of existence. The supple satin channels through the depths of time. No fear or feeling of what's near. A reflection of the moon races with the stars as the river runs it's path. It flows with out direction or selfishness but with the freedom of the clouds in the sky. No boundaries, no limitations. Just pure liberation. Without thought and emotion as the rocks pierce it's skin. The horizon is it's guide to a future set forth to cleanse what it cant do independently. No concept of life or time. IT JUST IS!...Ju-San.

2013

Here is one I wrote in 2013 on this day before having my Poetry page.

Another day has fallen as the silhouette of the night rest in silence. The sounds of the days past echoes in the minds of those active in happiness. Grasp the moments of that fine memory that has yet to forget the thoughts in your mind. For it is days that appear gray that should be left behind. The wind sings as the trees dance in a melody unheard. Take this time to listen to the sounds of unspoken words.Sleep well tonight without regrets or something not said. The heart beats in a rhythm as your dream might be your last in bed. Take this meaning to your own understanding for your personal gain. A breath of one is a breath of all, the endings are never the same. So farewell to you for my night has now found conclusion. My ending is in peace, so next time we meet we can voice our reason. Ju-San...

_____

_____

_____

_____

_____

_____

_____

_____

_____

_____

_____

August 22,2017

My daily inspiration: People say think outside the box. I say if you think outside the box then you'll never know what beauty holds inside. But if you stay thinking inside the box then you'll never know about what life truly has to offer on the outside. I say, KICK THE SHIT out of that damn box out of your way. The box limits your mind and restricts your vision. The box holds all the negativity and bad energy constricted in one area. When do we take charge to say "Ef that"!? NO MORE RESTRICTIONS, NO MORE LIMITATIONS. Where is your 👆 ☞ Faith 🖖 👉 in yourself? BELIEVE! Here's a quote I wrote some time ago," If you believe you can achieve, you will succeed. With success you are victorious"! Doesn't matter the quantity so as long as you kick the "box" out of your vision that holds so much life's BS. The quality will happen naturally. In conclusion, a Bruce Lee quote: "It is like a finger pointing it's way to the sky. Don't concentrate on the finger or you will miss all of that heavenly glory"! Just for you Faith Lee...this is your inspiration...Ju-San

August 28,2016 (New Orleans-Esplanade and Frenchman) Uber

Can we walk together as strangers and sore through time and talk about useless things? Enjoy a moment on the soft prickled grass and look at what's to be seen. Feel Gods breath breathe through our hair as the cotton sky surrounds us everywhere. Let us strangers chat for a minute and remember for a moment who we are not. This chess game awaits for you to sit and take a spot. Running through the fields liberated without worries or concerns, watching you swaying back and forth in a dance of nothing you've yearned. Can we sing a melody in a soft unspoken hymn of compound expression from within? I've already written the notes for all or any musical lessons to be whistled. Sir, may I help you cross the street? A short conversation is appreciated from your eyes. The tree branch leaves are conversing with each other by its side. Barefoot on this warm cement from a long night of City lights.(song I'm currently listening to by the White Stripes). Walking away from what's behind before walking through my hotel door. What would you ask of me as we look upon the sad and happy eyes of all the passer bys who seem to be in their own world with no concern of what surrounds their being. A question with no mark just an uncertain response. These tired eyes yawn in an unrested time. My moment is gone but will return as i unwind. Blinks his eyes, maybe a nap in a dime...Ju-San

June 17,2018

Pierce the wind with hollow stones. Breaking through the light.
Numb is the empty soul, with death as near as night.
Closing thoughts without the fear the eyes will close astray.
Sing this song with words along the base will breath always.
With haste away, you shall decay for time you cannot flee.
Look inside my face denies nothing of my feeling.
Stand with legs and un-grasped hand, you fall with tremble stance.
Your pavements faced with unmarked grave, you never had a chance.
Spirit flies with undenied the body has died in grief.
Hollow soul his torments cold, this tree has shaken leaf.
It's dark inside with box aligned you share this home of crown.
Nails of ten are pierced within, you may never be found.
Enjoy your stay of mournful play, residence you will remain.
No pillow for comfort or blanket for warmth, what is your name? ...Ju-San

---

June 20, 2018

The phantoms will to perform an act of kindness in conducted form.

He's worn this mask that has you blinded of who is really torn.

Love in heaven the man has felt nothing less for you.

Will you grant him the chance for a dance of romance, songs in moments cue!?

You spin in a gentle motion to express your feelings you hath.

Quite the same it will remain, never to leave me, in the wrong path.

We dance with the angels for a melody of birds in notes of beautiful chime.

Fingers tipped with grasp unlocked for the bell will ring in time.

The ghost has longed for a companion he has fought for in present past away.

He dies with a broken heart that his mind can't seem to bare, this moment he has now slept in fray ... Ju-San

December 6, 2017

The life and death of an unspoken man who has lived some of his life in darkness of his own abuse. The venom was of great importance that entered into the soul of your own frailty. Living and sleeping in a tired room. Were the tears not enough when your own reflection walked toward you without grudge, hate or judgement? Only the simple yearn for your own embrace.

And yet here we are, feeble without words or expression. No movement without a cry afar.

You are silent more so now then before. Have the words escaped through the open door, heavy weighted to the endless floor? No where to be found for his mind is now gone.

How can you teach through silence? By vision itself to see how he lays not awake or asleep. He has fallen again! We collaborated our thoughts unspoken to his truth but he never spoke before with only time that he refused.

The room is mildly cold and sullen as he gives a blank stare. His mind is unaware of what is this silhouette that he glares.

Your presence is exclusive to your right as we share an unholy drink tonight. Praying for salvation!

A production of a sad story without its cast as i try to dialogue this scene. He forgot his lines!

Your hands are the sandpapers of manual labor that built your life with black pepper hair, smooth like the salty ocean, vast in depth without quarrels in strife.

My tears is the ink to these words that are not clear as your eyes not see that of my reflection is of you.

You have now passed through your time as you've released your last breath that you've been able to muster leaving behind what is yours.

A son of incompleteness! Left behind once again with no final words of wisdom or encouragement!!!

To my father Julio Alamo Sanchez(Nov.5,2017 RIP)...Ju-San!

_____

_____

_____

_____

_____

_____

_____

February 18,2015

At this very moment what are you feeling? Perhaps happy, glad, content? Maybe depressed, upset, emptiness, or lament? What triggers this feeling that is consuming you internally? What is it that brings you joy in your heart unconditionally? Money, children, good job, nice home? AHHH, all the fine things in life. Happiness without strife! Hmmmm, as i raise my brow at this moment here and now i can not figure out why do you still complain? A stasis of complete, what? I refrain from speaking. It is a question for you and none other then several few who is maybe bothered by my own "not making any sense" conceptual notion. Well, it is only a question of thought. Time and time again i have fought to understand what my eyes sought out before me. Maybe i speak in parables...This is not directed to anyone personally, its just for you to open your eyes and maybe see what you are missing. Now if you are one of those that fall in the 2nd and 3rd line, well stop making excuses and get off your ass and make something happen. Remember, in this world you are one, but to one you are the world!...Ju-San

February 18, 2015

An old man is at a city park practicing his Tai Chi Chuan. Gentle as the sky is calm. He is approached by a young lad at a distance. He tries to hide his true motive in the silhouette of the trees. Entrigued by the old mans gentle and soft movments his curiosity expands. His approach is patient with an indirect question. The old man is aware of the young mind as he continues to practice his exercise. The young man finally makes his encounter and to much of the latters surprise, the old man says with a old crows voice "a lifetime"! Perplexed and bewildered the young man ask, how did you know what i was going to ask? The old man replies, "You can spend a lifetime searching for the truth and never find it, but that time was never wasted for an open and empty mind is enlighted to was is already true to its nature". The young man is confused but yet he felt an immediate cleanse as he walks away lighter in his burden. When he finally understood the concept he attempted to ask another question to the old mans response. What is my purpose in life? Your purpose is to have no purpose and JUST LIVE, the old man says. If you give yourself a purpose you limit yourself of your full capability and potential. River water has no destination, no thought or question. IT JUST IS! A tiger does not think consciously of when it will feed, IT JUST DOES! In deep thought of the old mans words he turns away as a gust of wind kisses his face. When he turns back he notices that the old man is gone and a whisper to his ears echoes, JUST BE!...Ju-San

February 24,2016

Have you ever wondered who you are? Who you really are? By far no one can say they do know. That shows how much we pay attention to the person in the mirror without mention. We are so caught up in today's society of such haste that we waste ourselves by daily routine. Where's the pause for a breath of our own? Bestowed upon to us is routine, what you have to do! Only a few of us will STOP and enjoy our own breath rather then breathing for what's been mechanically designed in our minds by routinely doing the same thing redundantly. Here comes the excuses of this and that is the reason. What a treason to your own essence. Where is the enjoyment of "quality time"? No need to define the meaning! I'm sure you all get it! Hey man, this is just a random thought that is fought in my mind. At times I try to make the change but hey, without the support its not the same. I never stopped trying though...Ju-San

February 25,2017

I have seen something that i haven't seen in almost 3 decades. A life that i once knew that only a few still remains to see as i played in the arcade.

The houses that i viewed where lived the few that i remembered as i walk into a warmth of no a.c. that reminds me of ME. How i live now without the coolness to budget of yup, that a.c.

I have seen this old man who once had his hands in his work of all day with no play to support in his own way. Yeeeah, I kinda see that he's into the same style of hats that i wear. He's cooler more then me because he has stories with great memories that i have yet begun TO BE.

Breakfast time has arrived as she cooks with this simple lean to the side as the age has overwhelmed her days. Noticed as i smell the eggs and ham as well as mine. Cooked the same way.

I was recently told from a young man who clearly now stands 1 foot 4 above my hand when reached above my head. That he looked up to me when we were young. But now i clearly see that i look up to him in height now just for fun.

Now this special girl is the light of the party as i can hardly begin to gather the notion of what was in the potion when she was conceived. She is nutty and wild with a sailors smile as she dances before me.

Our little artist has lost some motivation to pencil the colors of artistic innovation. She has a good eye for the sketch of detailed lines of profound depth. Take a step back and watch with me as i show you life in 3-D. Then you will see all of life's true poetry of colored shades in you, you'll see!

You have shaven sides of self expression without ever taken a course or lesson. You express yourself as you are with the happiness and smile like the stars. But with a sadness of inner being. I am here for you if you need to lean for a few minutes to gather your thoughts that you have constantly fought. You are not alone. I have been there too. Might be a different reason or setting but the sadness is still the same in truth. So refer to the 4th line as i sentence a visit with you for a little time.

These are all true stories of my recent visit in Chicago. Family member's that ive grown up with and some that i just met for the first time. For the rest of you's i will get you in a writing on my next visit...Ju-San

February 25,2017

How can you hear the silence that screams innuendos without a word spoken out!? Inside the dainty eyes, it bursts out its vocals in a stream of tears that flows down the rivers of sorrow. You've crashed down to your knees reaching out for forgiveness. No one is there! Willingness devoured by the shadow of guilt that consumes you. Your plea is in-suffice but a bargain not to ignore. Bleed your words, before you drown to shore. Is this but a dream of a lucid character that's clearly misunderstood? Perhaps a precise document of an unwritten story of words defined in a rhyme of nothing more then a blind sentence. Unable to exclaim the point. You've gestured in the middle of disbelief with your right hand of partial dominance. Illustration at its best! Continuing to mock me with the rest of the surrounding. The way is directed without direction...Ju-San

These words are illusions coming out of my head,
Spilling from the universe I feel cursed again.
Time waits for no one when comes the end,
If I continue to write when will I begin?
A friend told me once that life is laughter,
Here is what I said a few minutes after.
This I say to you in a soliloquy of words,
If I continue to write when will my letters be heard?
Dark does not write the words on this page,
Moments of silence is what I feel some days.
The scarlet fades in the inner hour glass,
Must keep on writing or the time will pass.
Is my head filled with this magnitude of lies?
Or am I just a soul waiting to pass by?
The lines of the elegy get smaller by day,
Must continue writing what I feel he say.
I am not trying to mock my own thoughts,
I'm just running out of time by the hands of the clock.
So forgive me now if I don't share the same humor,
Can't wait until the end, wish it would come sooner.
You might think this poem is merely on death,
I assure you this is not for a rest.
If I wrote the words that the others breath,
Thee will be plenty of me to be seen.
My dirge is a song of mournful play,
I don't expect for you to understand some things I say.
Back to the beginning is where I will end,
These words are illusions coming out of my head...Ju-San

_____

_____

_____

_____

_____

_____

January 5,2015

It's been a while but this ones from the other night when the weather was bad. Hope you enjoy!

I hear "Riviere" in my Def-tone echoed ear. Who's footsteps do I hear up there? Walking silently and patiently on the beams of stability. Only for the rot to creek. The high winds speak in a whisper of falling leaves. Branched to a scratching window. Silhouette of an eerie speech of wordless vowels. The clock is still ticking here and now. Muster breaths are deep and constant, the eyes are heavy in time. You hear yourself speak in the gray of what matters, these words are truly mine. It is now quiet as the wind dissolves away. No one to speak to or hear my dirge at play. An elegy of a compound melody, my notes for you to read. Vanished as unseen spoken dreams, hunger for your feed...Ju-San

July 14,2016

Something I want you all to do today! With all the crisis and issues that have been bestowed upon us all, take a min, stop what you're doing, tell friends and family that you love them, take a walk outside, enjoy the sun on your face and smell the fresh air and JUST BREATH for a moment! Help a stranger, give to the homeless, take a different path home, show some courtesy, call an old friend, be courageous but not foolish, play hooky. We all need that childish moment. Go watch a comedy or sad movie. Its ok to laugh and cry. Cleansing is necessary. Light a candle for a loved one. Take a moment for a prayer. Words are always heard. Indulge a little. But most importantly, BE HAPPY! Silence your mind and enjoy that very moment that we all have been blessed with. Ty...Ju-San

_____

_____

_____

_____

_____

_____

_____

_____

_____

_____

_____

_____

_____

July 29,2016

He reaches for the dade as he sinks into the dark drowning pool of merciless sorrow. The advance of prolific energy to rid of his being. No one or two to be seen as he moves forth in a lean. The strings are short with no movement of just! This is the time and moment he feels he must drive into his plain of shroud. Wrapped in agony of a bloody vain. The voice isn't heard of words out loud. The latter is lucid as he's sinking in his own demise!...Ju-San

_____

_____

_____

_____

_____

_____

_____

_____

_____

_____

_____

_____

_____

_____

_____

_____

_____

July 8, 2016

It's hard to force a smile without feeling the hurt in your face. Never would you have thought that you would be such a disgrace. On the pavement you have fallen once again, buckled in pain. Mother can't fix this. Their is no gain but tears again and again. What have you done? You ask! The liquor is dry in the flask. It's what I didn't do. He slurs his reply. Time will prove its theory correct without a shy moment. The balance is broken! The convenience is an inconvenience. None of this makes sense. Tell me again what has happened?!? Pointless! No words will rectify this madness for it is to late. The feeling has settled in, the broken heart can not mend. You've lost and now it has been... Done! No more friend! This tension builds high! Steam sweats down the brow to his eyes. Time! Why this...Time?!? It'll all be forgotten and moved on. The care is now and will be soon long and gone. Imprisoned to your own cell. No one to call upon. The key sits on the small window sill. Somber is the sky. No release for your screams. Who would hear? You want to feel this agony to pay for your dues. This is my fault! Can not undo! Torn and self chastised, you embrace the pain. It's your own company. CEO to your own business. You're own creation!...Ju-San

_____

_____

_____

_____

_____

_____

_____

_____

_____

_____

June 13,2015

Ahhh, finally a moment of quiet walls. Nothing for you to say. But hear and know all. Our words echoes through as a sign of my presence. Voiced in musical notes without a lesson. Play with my mind as an instrument of puppets. Strings attached but the master has cut it. Let go as eyes should see. You've trapped me inside of dark serenity. Shhh, did you hear that??? The mouse has much to say in this house of dark and gray. Candles lit to watch a step. The hot wax of pain as it wept. The door shuts with much to say. Keep it lock for its better this way. If I shall return for another meet, be sure to keep the kettle hot for tea...Ju-San

June 16,2015

I enjoy using renaissance grammar...still in practice.

Bella, Oh Bella where art thou Bella? I yearn for your sweet embrace with tears of sorrow on my face. As thee so far away I plee to the gods for your presence to stay. Return a gesture with your fine hand, as tasteful wine on your lips I demand. So stare not I into your pupils I fly, in your gaze of piercing eyes. As I return to thee with flowers in my hand, whatever your wish is surely my demand. Forget me not in your other life I despise, if happiness is what you live, this I will not deny. I wander to through time in hopes for peace. I can not find what I truly seek...Ju-San

June 29,2016

What must we do to solidify the truth? The moments in our lives that we must come to realize and wonder "who we are"?! By far we have forgotten our being of existence. Take time to listen to your inner voice without listening with deaf ears. Do you fear the outcome, or do you plan to outrun what you fear? Lets logic the words together in a compound sentence that makes sense! As lucid as we must express ourselves with hence, your gut feeling! Silence your mind, clear your thoughts, and take a moment to look at your world. It is a reflection of who YOU are. Itll stare back with how you view it. Do not deceive your perception with clouded thoughts. It is a struggle that you will learn, in spite of what you have fought. Be fluid in your decision making but yet reasonable. Judge without judgement! Know before you speak or set and opinion! Give without expectancy! Receive to pay it forward! Teach without a lesson, but acknowledge limitations! Be, before and after, but never in-between! You must grow with life and blossom! Dont regret your regrets, because it doesnt regret in return! Will you follow your mind into a universal state of time? A time to just Be! So i ask, where is your truth! Go seek it, though it can take an un-wasted lifetime!..Ju-San

June 9,2015

To <u>Victor Rivera</u>, We all are going through something negative in our lives. Weather its finances, children our job or with our wives.(not mine, I'm divorced...lol). We wake up in hopes that it'll be a better and brighter day, well let's just say that is solely up to you. Be the fighter that we all know you are. Mickey(Rocky) once said," if you think good, you'll do good"! Whatever brings you down, think of what you have and make it a happy frown. You have your friends, family, children and most importantly your health. There's not enough wealth in this world better than that. Face the sun in the morning and say "I WILL CONQUER ALL MY FEARS AND ISSUES AND PREVAIL. The rest will follow through. You will smell the roses like a king with hail. Think of what makes you laugh, happy and smile cuz all the while someone else is worst off. That will be your guide to Serenity, Humility and Tranquility! My brother you've had a rough patch growing up but you still walk amongst the living. But none the less a patch that has fixed the hole that has been bestowed on you... Walk on my friend! Ju-San.

March 12,2018

You are racing with your shadow but in which direction? To or fro!?(In his slow inner tone) Steady! Steady now! Pace yourself! The wind is pushing. It's getting harder to go. (Stumbles on his hands and knees) Face down his nose bleeds. The taste of his own blood weakens his spirit. A mirage he sees forth musters his curiosity. What is in sight can not be grasped. WAIT! He yells in trembled voice of eagerness. The transparent image sways as the grass in the nearby brush. He stands on his feet, with great determination he commences to walk forward. Time is setting against him. MOVE! MOVE YOUR LEGS DAMMIT! The breathless awaits in transparency. The latter races forth against the conjunction of pavement and wind. He is directed north. Arrives to the point that nothing is there but the award that he has won the race against his own fear...Ju-San

March 24, 2015

I touch the moon with my hands, As i pierce through the clouded sky. The Stars shape steps as I walk with a naked eye. Ambient energy echoes to my ears, For the sound of light I welcome with no fear. Hold me high to dade of sky, My journey is within grasp. Absence of color as its laps. Moon drops burst in a vibrant pose, the smell of flowered dustis nosed. Lingering to a charades of words unspokenBleeding sky will deny me entry without token. These days, moments are silent as the sky is full. Whisper winds are settled and cooled. The background sings in silhouette, i breathe angrily in a cold sweat. Where did my echo cry? Sigh! He's pondering with grave thoughts on the lights that are dimmed. Fading in and out of delirium. I've been warranted without a court unable to answer as i retort. His expression perchance the possibility enhanced without voice. The night shadow is my cape unable to face my disgrace. While the glass beats, the heart seeps in scattered blood without love. Daylight falls in the hands of darkness as the sounds of crescendo stole my voice of innuendo with no likeness. The silence is loud in decibels heard from the dead resting in the clouds. What do you fear? What is absent and aware of what is near. Do i pay whats due to the blood of what burst from above? What has destroyed the bright light can not be redeemed. So it seems that i can not find my eyes to see the destruction in the sky. I did not see this coming...Ju-San

_____

_____

_____

_____

_____

_____

_____

_____

March 25,2018

So many words I want to say to you but the higher in power
have limited me to say only a few. How does one ask or tell to
keep silent? At this moment the beneficiary has benefited for
her highness. Time and time has passed me by only for you to
take back what is rightfully mine. Your selfishness has led you
to believe that it is not age appropriate for her to conceive in
her mind the truth!? So now again i must play by your rules
and silence what is aloof in my being. Do you fear that the open
words spoken from innocence could devastate the guardian? In
all actuality you both guard in sin by keeping your honesty paper
thin. You have stolen my right from me as you smile and walk
away from my own tragedy. I have tried to muster the vowels with
out cursing. Yet, I swear a vow in sane mind not to go insane at
this time. My past predictions have made itself noticed. But know
this, that my words are not a note in this page. I will sentence my
confession to those who judge in court. Upon completion i will
have left on the side with no remorse...Ju-San

May 10,2016

Will you come running when you here the sound of the bell when his glory is upon us? A sound you will here from a distance and yearning for his sweetness to arrive. He will give you choices that will be hard to choose from. Mother taught you about his holiness and presence. Patient you stand and await his arrival. Without denial you have made a choice. His tune is played and heard by recognized sound from family all around. Do you deny his existence? Have you been denied his salvation? He comes when you scream his name out loud at your mercy. You are ready to pay your dues for his offer is unbearable. He will come if you believe and wait for your time. He comes alone as his disciples follow. He will repeat a familiar scripture to sound ears. Familiar for years and years. There is no book that truly explains who he is or the happiness he has bestowed upon us. Believe in him! Will you eat what he has offered as he gives with worn flesh of the cries he here's from the nest? Who is he, what's his name? WHO AM I? Take a guess!...Ju-San

May 10, 2016

An old monk walks on a road touched by the sun. He approaches a young priest. Without judgement or prejudice they sit together and have tea. Converse and appreciate each other's company. The young priest then ask, where are you headed sir? The old monk replies, where ever the Zephyr wind takes me! Confused on his response the young priest quietly sips his tea. Sincerity in the old monks eyes he asked the young priest, where have you been? The young priest answers with a patient response, ive been neither here or there but only where I've been in the moments. The old monk smiles with great ease. As time slowly approaches, the old monk says to the young priest, you can be somewhere and nowhere at the same time. But nowhere can be somewhere when you are there! As they finish their tea and gather their belongings, the old monk and young priest part ways...Ju-San

May 16, 2018

A mournful play of elegy for a self-contained binge,
His voice in thought of a wail he's fought, confines him in his sin.
Shackled underground not to set free,
Innocuous at heart, charged with all levels of degree.
Forgotten and astray, do I exist?
Starving for answers and a peaceful hold,
The body is lithe, mournful and cold.
This jargon used in supple tongue,
Yearns for light and his freedom.
Quis est que condemnet for my only soul,
Lacrimarum valle so how it flows.
Release these chains that has me in bind,
The skeletons key hangs in free time.
Do my eyes amiss what I see in sight?
My feeble bones lost in this unfair fight.
Binded to this wall, hitherto and space,
Sordid to the core, converse the judge in abate.
The jury will discuss, in sojourn of their time.
Patiently waiting my voice in mime...Ju-San

November 17,2015

Imprisoned without sin but given every reason to scream again.
You cant right this wrong with lyrics or songs but you can keep
in sight the anger inside only for so long. When every vowel
is pronounced in a foul syllable, taken under my breath. I've
imprisoned my words from speaking the truth. While the quarry
has been enquired by the enquiries of this man. Lets break the
silence of being silent again as my voice is my instrument trying
to instruct lament...though your words voice your conclusion. In a
way its pointless although you still remain nameless. So what now,
do I fold the night sky and bow? I guess for now I will continue
to let the scarlet bleed off my pen until or unless this happens
again. So for those of you that understand, well next time lets not
reminisce, lets remember...Ju-San

November 17, 2014

If your life was a season which would it be? Would it be Spring? A time of new beginnings? The past season is gone into a state of nothingness. This is YOUR time to start over with YOUR life. Your rebirth! Set new meaning and definition for yourself. Look forward to new growth as so does nature. Or would it be SUMMER? A time to blossom as a beautiful flower. This is the time to walk YOUR path. You've grown fully colored to your personality. MAKE YOUR WAY! Maybe it's Autumn?! Where all things should have fallen into place for yourself. This is the time of experience. Then is when you've exercised what you have learned in YOUR path and journey. But as all good and beautiful things, it all has to end in the Winter. Where life is gray and grave as so in death. But death is not all that bad. If we don't die and let go of our old selves how are we to learn and grow again and become better? Let free of all existence and Spring into new beginnings. Better to advance and never to stop. Do not let your mind expel imagination. Their is a Chinese adage from the Tao Te Ching. This is called "emptying your cup". Ask me and I will tell you what that means. So the question still stands. If your life was a season what would it be??? Well, lets just see...Ju-San

_____

_____

_____

_____

_____

_____

_____

_____

_____

_____

November 17.2014

As i rest myself i shall leave sojourn, i do not wield the urge to stay. As time counters to a place unknown, now i must walk and pray. For a safe return i must leave you now for my journey as just begun. The rhythm of sound is bold and bound, has not yet been sung. Echoes in my head as the trees break to sway. I fall in direction, dead is where it lays. The whispering winds are souls to my ears. My grasp cannot touch what hopes are near. If fear is what i know then my place is not whole. Your comfort, your sanity, how loud my screams. I cannot witness the echoes so it seems. Under the clouds the sky hangs bright. I see my reflection on the silk of the night. The ripples are wrinkles as the stone pierce through. Beaten by weakness his struggle is more than a few. Guidance he seeks for his road is lost. Affected by rage his whispers are soft. For his travel has commenced his legs dust free. Return to the place where he needs to be...Ju-San

November 17,2014

Somber night, pale moon light, this graveyard wreaks with death, wind speak in my ear, the warmth of someone's breath. Thoughts are playing with my head, I'm feeling a little confused, this reality is fading, acceptance is refused. Shadows play on the headstones grave, music is unsound, the raven's croak to the music notes, as his beak echoes the ground. The fog is settled as it blankets the graves, my heart beats in crave. No more in fear of what's been near, an experience of close death. Closer to the end, no longer to pretend, it was the warmth of my own breath. I'm still not clear of what whispered my ear, perhaps my fears aloud, the cold chill whines as it enters my spine, I'm covered in a shroud. Time does not exist, as my world is in mist, I will see you all too soon. I whisper a hymn, waiting for a friend, my song stained the moon...Ju-San

November 17,2014

I want to sit by the beach and watch the waves crash as it explores it's true nature when the time pass. Watch the birds play in the sky while children build sand castles wide and high. Just for a moment I would like too see the image of someone who I'm supposed to be. My reflection is naked and bare as the sun sets, I begin to stare high to the clouds as the Angels playfully rain out loud. Feel the cleansing pour down my face as all negativity and disgrace is washed away. Walking slowly towards my serenity, as I release all that's in me. My crying laughter fills beneath, As the strength fades from under my feet. Children are still playing as I think of praying inside my head, birds are laughing high an loud, echoes are being fed, but I'm too proud. Still sitting watching the sun melt in the sky, the fallen tears bleed from ours eyes. Clouds absorb all the false hope as the hands lifts you blind waking up with a slight choke. WAS THIS REAL OR WAS I DREAMING??? Something touched me that is unknown to familiarity, feet flat in the sand but this does not scare me. The scene was empty with no child at play, the sky was alone with no birds laughing away. The waves still crash as lightning above my head, with a slight notice of sand castle that fed, MY CURIOSITY. Am I enlightened to foresee that my life is clear and free? Or was this a dream of something I didn't see? Ju-San...

_____

_____

_____

_____

_____

_____

_____

_____

FINALE

I have learned through my mistakes, experiences and struggles to let go of certain things in life. Things beyond my control. Things I cannot change.

Please do not judge or state an opinion especially about me without never knowing the whole truth.

What was learned through these unfortunate times?

Throughout the years I've understood more and more about myself as time passes by. Before it was easier to explain what I am rather than who I am.

We face challenges in life that may be difficult or do not make any sense.

It will test YOU and your morals and your human nature.

How you respond to such exam will define something about you and your character.

Study life! Study people! Study nature! Study time! I don't mean actual time on the clock I mean the essence of the moments past. Those moment when actions happen and how quickly you will respond and with what commitment will you commit to!?

I didn't have the luxury to have both parents, role models, mentors, and so on to help guide me in a right path. Some came and left. My mother tried her hardest and suffered on as well. I learned by observation, the streets, and through other people who just happened to be on the same journey.

Now that you have walked in my mind maybe you will now understand just a little of who I am and why I am the way I am. I came up in a different place at a different time and been through things that you will hopefully never experience.

So, I will leave you with this as a guide...

Ignore the ignorant but understand their lack of knowledge.

Be humble! Stay true to yourself!

Define who you are by your definition, not others.

Walk a path by your choice, not others.

Give, but do not take what is not given. It's a constant circle.

Be aware of what surrounds you not just in front. What you think you see in front might not be real. True words from others are revealed behind you.

Believe in yourself and your gut instinct. Nothing is more natural.

Speak less, listen more!

"Take" time for yourself, friends and family. Don't "make" time. Time already exists.

Exercise your mind and body for longevity and good health.

Defend yourself when left with no other choice is an option.

Always help other in need. You might need it one day also.

Read some good books. It'll expand your vocabulary and imagination.

Practice and Patience(Trinity), it will help you to move forward.

Inspire and Motivate!

Do not judge on first impression. Give people time to display who they really are.

Choose your words carefully. One word can change the entire outcome.

If you want to do something, DO IT! No excuses. Do not let anyone or anything deprive you from happiness.

Respect yourself and others.

Always save for a rainy day. And believe me, it rains.

Communicate with your siblings and your parents. At the end of the day we are what you have left when everyone else leaves you stranded.

Live with no past regrets. You can't change what's already been done but you can prepare by learning from your mistakes for a better future.

"Life is a gift, that's why it's called the present". [?]

Never sleep angry. It is very unhealthy.

Always excel.

ALWAYS know facts before making any judgement and/or opinion.

Have faith in GOD. There is a reason all things happen. Everything has its place.

Never give all your trust to ANYONE. Being naïve and gullible are your enemy.

Do not just settle for anyone or anything because it is there and convenient. There is much more out there to witness and experience.

Raven, you have always put everything else before yourself. Take time for YOU. All other things can wait. And, give her a chance. She didn't ask for this or to be here. A chance is all that I ask. You know who I'm talking about.

Always go above and beyond. The outcome will be your greatest reward.

If you can not change it, why worry about it. It'll work itself out.

NEVER lie! Always be honest no matter the situation and outcome.

Lyana, I might not be there 100% in your life, but you are in mine. So, from me to you, believe half of what you see and none of what you hear. Not everything is of what it seems.

Forget what you think you know, acknowledge what you truly understand. This will make sense in time.

ALWAYS stay focused and have good balance.

When there is too much noise, scrambled thoughts, confusion, uncertainties, anxiety, stress etc…Take a moment to breath and SILENCE YOUR MIND! (Tristan)

We might not always have agreed and bumped heads but know all I ever wanted for you is to be happy and let me help you. I never loved you any less than your siblings. You too are stronger than you know. Especially when you hit me with your right punch… lol (Nessy)

And last but not least, your mind should be a game of chess. ALWAYS think steps ahead.

These are my own personal advice to you that may help you on your journey. These are free words so please accept my gift.

If I have forgotten to tell you something, this is ok. You will learn the rest on our own. Mistakes and defeat will be your best teacher in life. You must learn from them.

In conclusion,
Girls,

Don't just believe any BS that the boys tell you. Use your common sense. Do not accept any drinks from them unless you saw the server make it or pop the top and hand it to you. They can be stupid at times but realize that they too are learning and trying to find their way.

They like to be impressive, show off and talk shite (British way of saying shit… pronounced like "shight" lol…Delicia Boudeaux) but not all are so bad. Give them time. We can be a little slow. It's the turtle that won the race though. HAHAHA

And to my only son,

You are very special. You see things in ways that we cannot relate to.

In case I'm not around to show you, ALWAYS respect people and especially women. Open the door for them, pull out the chair when she is to be seated. Rub her back, cook dinner if you are home first, defend her honor, and please whatever you do, LISTEN to her because she will ask you to repeat it and more importantly DO NOT ARGUE WITH HER. YOU WILL NOT WIN!!!

And to my mother,

I know you tried your best and I love and thank you for that. Had we not been through the things we have, who knows where I will be.

It has molded me into the person that I am today. THANK YOU.

Mother, I want you to remember that we all have our demons and are not perfect. Have faith in Sammy and Emily. They too have been through their share of lost. We are no better than anyone else. They will come around sooner or later...Hopefully sooner. HEHE

The moment has come to end this ride. A journey in mind, space and time.

You have learned a little of what pains my heart, this will end soon here is the start...

And as my Trinity and Tristan always say,

"THANK YOU VERY MUCH, THE END!"

I love you all dearly,

Dad

THANK YOU

A special thanks to Time, Life, and Experiences that has brought me to this place of wisdom and knowledge and molded me into the person that I am today. Without you who knows where I will be.Thank You"...Ju-San

Printed in the United States
By Bookmasters